Twelve Commandments
For People
Who Work With People

By Ann T. White, Ed.D.

Edited by Frances C. Helms

Published by Threadgill Press, Cowpens, S.C.

Published by Threadgill Press, Drawer 1019,
Cowpens, S.C. 29330

ISBN 0-9672781-0-4
Printed in USA

Library of Congress Catalog Card Number:
99-94591

Dedication

This book is dedicated to my first husband William, who has seen me through three children, two careers and numerous garden crops, from whence comes my title "Turnip Queen," but that is another story.

This book also is dedicated to my children, Lori Gleason and Bill and Joel White, who are my biggest bucket-fillers and who serve as my moral compass.

Additionally, this book is dedicated to the memory of my mother, Idell Parker Threadgill, an amazing human being, who was always able to keep her sense of humor even in the worst of times.

Finally, this book is dedicated to the thousands of professional people who have kindly invited me to speak to them, to share my knowledge and more than a few laughs, and who asked me to put into writing my philosophy for success in the workplace.

God bless you all.

Contents

Acknowledgements

This book is about teamwork. It is also a result of teamwork. Numerous people have helped, assisted and encouraged me in the writing of this book. First and foremost I am indebted to my colleague and good friend Frances Helms for editing this book. Frances spent many hours trying to make sense of my writings, tapes and ramblings. During the course of assisting me she fell and seriously injured her knee. Although, she was in much pain, she kept her wonderful sense of humor and continued to uplift my spirits throughout the arduous process of trying to put the information in this book in an understandable, informative and enjoyable form.

I am grateful also to my close friends Carol Ratzlaff and Ginger Cox for proofreading the copy and offering suggestions that I think improved the book. Both of these friends have enriched my life in many ways. If you find errors in the book. They are <u>not</u> responsible for them. I am.

Additionally, I am fortunate to have two dear friends, Nancy and Allen Atkins, who have kept my five-year-old computer running, even though, I frequently messed it up. They are also responsible for the layout of the book.

I am also thankful to my son-in-law David Gleason who asked me everytime I saw him-**"When are you going to finish that book?"** A big thank you is also extended to my lifelong friend Judy Weber, who has traveled with me and sold enough of my posters and tapes so that I could take time from my speaking schedule to work on this book.

To the thousands of people, who have listened to my speeches, written me encouraging notes and told others about me, **THANK YOU!**

Finally, I would be amiss if I did not acknowledge the support of my family, who has always stood beside me in all my endeavors.

Chapter One
Why You Should Read This Book

Teamwork. It's a simple word, but a complex concept. Unless you are your own boss, as well as your only employee, and your success or failure does not depend on the cooperation or support of anyone else, you need to become an expert on teamwork. People who work with people must learn to interact, to share the load, to encourage when discouragement threatens, to know when to talk and when to be quiet and when to laugh and when to be serious, to intuit the proper time to lead and the appropriate time to follow.

In my first career as a teacher and then a school administrator, teamwork was integral to ensuring the success not only of the individual student but also of the entire school system. When I "recareered," the term I prefer to use to describe my retirement from education and subsequent emergence as a humorist and motivational speaker for a variety of professional groups, I realized anew the importance of teamwork in all aspects of every workplace. That is why I developed the "Twelve Commandments For People Who Work With People," and why I stress humor in the process of observing these commandments.

Some people have told me that I frequently seem more like a standup comedian than a professional speaker, but that is part of my strategy. People rush to share jokes with friends; if it's funny, they'll repeat it. For that reason my company, "Laugh and Learn With Ann White," came into being. I want people to share what I tell them, to spread the word, to become part of my team and to form teams of their own, laughing as they learn.

A couple of years ago, the chief executive officer of a Fortune 500 company was widely lauded for espousing fun in the workplace. His philosophy was that if people enjoy coming to work, as a byproduct they will have fewer lost work days as well as increased productivity. Subsequent studies of his company's records proved the validity of his theory. More recently, the management of Southwest Airlines has made a reputation for sponsoring companywide contests and celebrations at the drop of a hat, for encouraging employees to have fun and to enjoy their work. In the process, Southwest's enthusiastic employees have transformed their company into one of the best run, most efficient and most profitable businesses — and not just among airlines — in the United States.

Another successful duo who believe in the importance of humor in the workplace are Ben Cohen and Jerry Greenfield. Better known simply as Ben and Jerry, the ice cream gurus from Vermont firmly believe in having fun, making money and giving much of the latter away to good causes — and pretty much in that order. You can get a taste (pun intended) of their penchant for fun simply by checking the names of some of their ice cream flavors: Cherry Garcia in tribute to the Grateful Dead's own Jerry Garcia; Chunky Monkey for a frozen yogurt; and the new flavor of Bovinity Divinity, consisting of white fudge cows swirled with white chocolate ice cream and dark fudge cows — a perfect pick for someone from a town named Cowpens.

But you don't have to be part of a multimillion-dollar organization to encourage a little on-the-job laughter. A Spartanburg County, South Carolina, school superintendent recently hired a public relations director to whom he stressed the necessity of fomenting better public relations inside the organization, and thus began at least a monthly round of nonsense designed to give people enjoyable breaks from serious duties. For example, staffers found personalized Valentine "boxes" posted on doors, encouraging them to rediscover "the inner child" and exchange holiday greetings; followed by a whimsical invitation to a ham biscuit breakfast; then a "bunny" delivering Easter candies; an intercom announcement concerning bagel treats at morning break; a watermelon slicing at the end of a hot summer day; and various other informal get-togethers designed to allow busy people a few pressure-free minutes to get to know each other better. Soon, staffers were asking, "What do we get to do next month?" and looking forward to thoughtful but simple and inexpensive surprises. They had begun to feel like part of a family or team, which was the serious intent behind the seeming foolishness.

Another innovative public relations tool was employed by a small publishing company: an office cookout every Friday at noon during the summer. The owner sprang for a picnic table, an outdoor grill, food supplies and an extra-long extension cord for the switchboard phone. The result? Everybody who visited the office on Friday was treated to an informal lunch, and the staff soon became the envy of the entire professional neighborhood. After an hour or so on the patio, everybody returned to work happy and refreshed, feeling they had started the weekend early and more than willing to work a little harder whenever necessary to meet deadlines. The management's expenditures, never much, were repaid many times over, and in ways that might not have been foreseen by anyone without a sense of humor and/or enjoyment in his or her work.

I have always believed the development of a sense of humor and a feeling of enjoyment to be integral to any job. I also believe in using as many personal illustrations as possible when speaking to any group. I share my life and my experiences in hopes that someone can use what I have learned for his or her own benefit. By employing humor in my presentations, I make personal connections: the first step toward building a team.

To help you make a personal connection with me as you read this book, let me tell you that I was born at home in a haunted house in Cherokee County,

South Carolina, and no, it reputedly was already haunted *before* I made my appearance. I never encountered any ghosts, but perhaps that was because we moved before I was old enough to know one if I saw one.

I began my education at Cross Roads Elementary School, one of the last one-room schools in the state, with just one teacher for thirty students in grades one through seven. When I started school, there were only three students in the first grade — my cousin Nancy, a boy called Little Eb (his father was Big Eb, naturally), and me. This was in the days when most school children saved Blue Horse coupons. For those of you who have never heard of Blue Horse coupons, they were found on notebook paper, composition books and other paper supplies which children of that day bought for school. I dreamed of saving enough Blue Horse coupons to get a bicycle, although I'm sure it would have required thousands and thousands, but my cousin Nancy didn't aim quite so high. She set a more achievable goal of saving enough coupons for a Blue Horse "beanie," which she eventually got. She was so proud of that beanie that she never took it off her head. She even wore it while using the bathroom, which was a non-plumbed one-seater located outside the school. For some reason, one day after using the facility, Nancy turned around and peered down into the toilet. You guessed it! To her dismay, the prized beanie fell off her head. She called me to come and help her try to retrieve her beanie, and we spent an hour and broke a couple dozen sticks in the futile attempt. I don't know to this day what we would have done had we been successful. Surely we didn't think we could have put that beanie back on Nancy's head! But she knew she had someone she could call on to help her with any problem and to commiserate with her over any loss. We were a team.

When we completed third grade, the administration closed Cross Roads School and transferred its students to Clifton Elementary, a large, three-story building. We were not readily accepted by the Clifton students, who looked down on us because we came from farm families while they lived in a thriving textile village. They called us "dirt daubers," treated us as though we were not as smart as they were, and, for the first time, caused me to learn the importance of staying focused, regardless of the circumstances. In the face of their determined rejection, I concentrated on my school work and studied hard. When I received my first report card at Clifton, I had made the honor roll, and the attitudes of some of my classmates began to change. When they saw that we could compete successfully with them, they began to accept us, and we began to feel more a part of their team and to share their school spirit.

Today, I live in Cowpens, South Carolina, about 65 miles south of Charlotte, North Carolina. The town got its name from the Revolutionary War's Battle of Cowpens where General Daniel Morgan's rebellious colonists defeated the British forces under Lt. Col. Banastre Tarleton, making this battle an important turning point in America's fight for freedom. Every local child is required to be able to recite this information at the drop of a hat — and not necessarily a Blue Horse beanie. The town is so small it has only one traffic light, and everybody knows everybody else. You know you're dealing with a long-time resident when you ask for directions and get the response, "Go to where the second traffic light used to be and turn left," and they can't believe you'll get lost. And you don't.

My home is the White House of Cowpens, in more ways than one. My first (and thus far, only) husband, William, is the Mayor of Cowpens. So, somewhat befittingly, in my mind anyway, I recorded the following message for our answering machine at home: "Hello, you have reached the White House. Bill and I can't come to the phone right now, but your message is important. Please talk after the tone, and we'll get back to you."

Some people didn't get it. And they got mad.

One evening our messages included this one: "I didn't call no #@*!!#@* White House and I don't want to talk to no *@#!!***! Pres-ee-dent! This here is supposed to be the mayor's house and I want to talk to him about my tax bill. *#@@!!+*! Forget it! I'll call City Hall. Maybe that *!**!!##* will be there. What is this *+!#, anyway?"

Suffice it to say, I changed the message. I quickly discerned that less tongue-in-cheek communication was required in this particular instance.

As in any position with a title, being First Lady of Cowpens could be an awesome responsibility, but I have learned not to take it too much to heart, or let it go too much to my head. The latter lesson was brought home to me during the first year after William was elected to office and I decided to ride with him in the Mighty Moo Parade.

For those of you who think I am making this up, every year on the third weekend of June, the Town of Cowpens hosts the Mighty Moo Festival, when crewmen from the first *U.S.S. Cowpens*, a World War II aircraft carrier nicknamed "The Mighty Moo," hold an annual reunion. On Saturday of that weekend, we stage The Mighty Moo Parade. My first year as First Lady of Cowpens was my first-ever opportunity to ride in a parade, and I really didn't know the protocol. But I did what I had seen the beauty queens do: I crawled up on the back of that shiny red convertible and I smiled and I waved graciously to everyone. We were almost at the end of the parade route when a little boy on the side of the street looked straight at me and yelled, "Hey! Miss Moo!" The crowd tittered. Actually, I heard a couple of belly laughs.

But it all went to prove that no matter how high and mighty you think you are, there is always some-body out there who can cut you down to size. As part of a team, you have to learn to deal with those people and to rise above it. And to keep smiling. And waving.

Recently I saw a sweatshirt with the caption "Genuine Antique—Been There, Done That, Can't Remember." I would prefer a shirt that reads: "Been There, Done That, Can't Forget."

I have witnessed what can be accomplished in a work environment where people agree on their mission, share the same goals and pull together to accomplish those aims and fulfill their mission. I have also been part of a workplace where the mission was fuzzy and people pulled in different directions trying to achieve their own personal agendas, with little regard for the overall welfare of the organization and the people it serves. After reflecting on the difference in the two environments and the ways that people related to each other, I developed the "Twelve Commandments for People Who Worked With People." This book is intended to entertain and educate you. I hope that my stories will give you a chuckle or two and lighten whatever burdens you are experiencing in your life. Much has been written about the physical and emotional benefits of laughter. It certainly makes me feel better, reduces the stress in my life and helps me survive everyday struggles. Laughter has been my best coping mechanism during change and transition. Often, when I start "sweating the small stuff," it helps me keep my perspective. Minnie Pearl once said that laughter is the hand of God on the shoulder of a troubled world. Personality conflicts, power struggles and communication problems can develop in any workplace. In these situations, laughter can help bring people together, build camaraderie and enhance teamwork. In addition to honing your sense of humor, this book is intended to help you understand the following commandments so that you can become a successful team- member in the workplace, can be a better role model for others and can develop a more positive, rewarding relationship with the people in your life.

Twelve Commandments
For People Who Work With People

1. Thou shalt love people.

2. SMILE.

3. Fill the "buckets" of others. Talk to them in such a way as to increase their self-esteem.

4. Exhibit a spirit of caring.

5. Display a "can do" attitude.

6. Beware! The "Chicken Little Syndrome" is contagious.

7. Strive for quality in all that you do.

8. Help people more; hassle people less.

9. Never be afraid to try to make things better.

10. <u>Train</u> your ears and <u>tame</u> your tongue.

11. Tell the truth. It's a lot easier to remember.

12. Practice the Golden Rule.

Chapter Two
Dead Cats And
How They Apply To You

Simplifying a great truth, *i.e.* translating noble phrases into language which great masses of people can easily understand, and offering examples to which they readily can relate, is not necessarily a simple task. However, I have found two words that help me deal with almost any situation life may present. Those two magical words are "dead cats."

Now, before the American Society for Prevention of Cruelty to Animals takes it the wrong way and puts me at the head of its Most Wanted list for apparently advocating the indiscriminating felling of felines, let me explain. This particular bit of wisdom came to me one hectic morning in 1986. You know the kind of day: It was a Monday, naturally, and I was running late, as usual, trying to get myself ready for a day of work in school administration and get out the door in time to drive my youngest child to school. My eldest child, Bill, all of 17 and a senior in high school, had left the house at 6:45, chauffeuring a big yellow school bus which the State of South Carolina, in its magnificent wisdom, then allowed 16-year-olds to drive. At 7 o'clock, in the middle of my makeup and breakfast (yes, I can do two things at once), the phone rang. I dashed for it, hoping to keep it from waking my husband, who had worked very late the night before.

"Mama, Mama, you have to help me!" a frantic voice begged.

"What is it, Bill?" I asked my son, a vision of his bus in a ditch turning my blood cold.

"I just picked up my first rider and he found a dead cat on my school bus," he responded. "What should I do with it?"

My response was immediate and to the point: "BILL, THROW IT OUT THE WINDOW."

That seemed to me to be the most expedient solution.

"No, Mama," he protested, drawing the word out into three syllables. "I can't throw it out the window. You have to come and get it."

"Bill, I'm in a big hurry," I said. "I have to get ready for work. I have to drive Joel to school. Just throw that cat out the window."

But he held firm. "No, Mama, I'm not going to throw the cat out the window. You have to come and get it."

Exasperated, I gave in. "Okay, son, where are you?"

The Twelve Commandments

"I'm up here at Brown's Store, where you turn left to go to Mayo," he replied.

"Okay, Bill. I'm going to tell you what to do. Take that cat off your bus and put it on the ground next to Brown's Store, and I'll send your daddy to get it."

My reasoning was that if you can't do the most expedient thing, sometimes you have to delegate.

So I went into the bedroom, shook William hard and said, "Get up, honey! Get up!"

Without opening his eyes, he mumbled, "What for?"

"You've got to get up right now and go and pick up a dead cat."

"What?" he asked unbelievingly, and one eye popped open.

"William, please, honey, I don't have time to explain," I urged in my sweetest tone of voice. "You just have to go and pick up this dead cat."

"Why me?"

"Because you're the only husband I have."

Grumbling, he got out of bed and pulled on his clothes while I gave him a quick explanation and directions to Brown's Store. We left the house about the same time, heading in opposite directions.

When I got home from work late that afternoon, William told me that he had driven his old pickup truck to retrieve that dead cat. Now you have to know that that old truck had cost less than our sons' go-cart, and with good reason. It ran, but that was about all you could say for it. Anyway, as William had driven north on Highway 110, he had had occasion to blow his horn. And it had stuck. So there he had been, driving up Highway 110, with the horn blasting all the way into the parking lot of Brown's Store. When he had braked to a stop and cut the engine, several people had come rushing out of the store.

"What's wrong?" they had inquired.

"Oh, I just came to pick up a dead cat. My wife sent me to get it," he had sheepishly explained.

And one woman had asked, "Well, if it's already dead, why were you blowing your horn so loud?"

This story represents a lot of what can happen to all of us every day on our jobs. We have all had unexpected situations arise which we have had to deal with to the best of our abilities. Can you honestly say that no one has ever thrown a dead cat on your desk, or around your neck, or at your feet? Maybe it was something you had never dealt with before, or maybe it was a dreaded recurring problem.

The only way I could deal with that particular dead cat was to call on others. I had my family there. I had my family who could help me with that situation. They helped me with the normal situations and they could help me with that unusual one.

I think that's how it has to be in the workplace. You have to be a family. You have to be a team — a team with members who are ready and willing to stand beside each other, a team that has the attitude, "We're in this together, and together we can do anything."

Everything we do, we must do with and through other people. I believe that if we work with others, regardless of the situation, regardless of what kind of dead cats come our way, we can accomplish miracles.

Chapter Three
Commandment No. 1: Love People

All human beings need to feel loved. All human
beings have this invisible sign around their necks
that begs, "Make me feel important." My favorite
description of love comes from the New Testament,
in the book of First Corinthians, where we read that
love is patient, love is kind, love endures, love edifies
and love forgets all wrongs.

In living with me for more than 30 years, my
husband William also has had to keep in mind the
words of another William (Shakespeare) in his Son-
net 116: "... Love is not love which alters when it
alteration finds, or bends with the remover to remove; oh, no! it is an ever fixed mark ... But bears it
out even to the edge of doom ..." Let me tell you now
that my William's love has extended beyond my bad

habits, fits of anger and sometimes roller coaster moods. I'm surprised he didn't leave me the first time I complained about his green pants and white suede shoes. But that calls for some explanation.

When I married William, he owned a pair of Easter egg-colored green linen pants that hung on him like a sheet wrapped around a telephone pole. He liked to wear those pants with a pair of white suede shoes that had gone out of style ten years earlier. Of course, having to smilingly accompany him while he was wearing that outfit was mortifying to me. So, one day I decided to fix those pants so he never again could wear them and embarrass my superior sense of fashion. What did I do? I ripped the seat out of his pants. Yes, I know now that that was pretty awful, but when I was twenty years old, it seemed like the right thing to do. Despite my intentional act of destruction, William stayed with me, continued to love me and to wear his white shoes. What happened to the pants? William's mother sewed the seat back in them, but he never wore them again.

That, my friends, is real love.

Scott Peck, in his book *The Road Less Traveled*, writes that "love is the will to extend oneself for the purpose of nurturing one's own or another's spiritual growth." Does this narrowly mean that you should attend a church with someone you love even though you personally dislike that particular church? No, I don't think so. I believe the sentiment is better illustrated by my good friend Carol, who attends performances of Shakespearean plays with her husband Alvin even though she doesn't like them. Or by my William, in never wearing those awful green pants again.

The Twelve Commandments

To Peck, all growth is spiritual. I think that Peck is trying to emphasize that love is not easy, it is often hard work, and it constitutes much more than infatuation, merely liking, or being sexually attracted to another person. After reading Peck's book, however, I immediately worried that I really didn't love a lot of people. In fact, I could think of only a few occasions when I had extended myself for the spiritual growth of another. I had once attended a Clemson University football game with my son Joel, and a cat show with my daughter, Lori — not at the same time, of course. After the football game, Joel told me that he had been embarrassed nearly to death because I had read a book instead of watching the action on the field. Okay, I suppose that extending oneself requires a bit more than merely sitting next to a sports enthusiast while he watches his favorite team. Real extension means watching every play, harassing the officials and yelling during all the appropriate intervals. Oh, yes, and leaving your book at home.

But, tell me, Dr. Peck, does going to a cat show when you'd rather be at home playing tiddly-winks really help the spiritual growth of your feline-loving daughter? Never mind. I already know the answer.

I also know that the importance of loving people extends beyond our mates, friends and family. I've already noted that all human beings need to feel loved; we need to love all people. That includes people in the workplace. Is it easy? No! Some people are a lot like kidney stones: They may lie quietly for long periods of time, then suddenly act up for no reason at all, causing you a lot of pain. If people in the workplace loved each other and were willing to extend themselves to help and assist each other, we could attain the highest of goals.

When I think of the workplace, I am reminded of a horrible experience when my boss, the superintendent of our school system, saw his career destroyed by politics — not the legislative variety, the interpersonal kind. This man had led the school district where I was employed for fifteen years, directing it to a position of prominence among South Carolina schools. His success, however, had inspired much jealousy among people who were prone to attempt to claim such distinctions for themselves, whether or not they deserved them. Those people eventually created so many problems for my boss that he departed, leaving behind a smoldering political battle that split the ranks of professionals in the school system, divided the support for the school system of many people in the community, and affected the educational process of thousands of innocent young people.

Those of us who had worked closely with this superintendent were saddened and depressed by his departure, but we had the awesome task of helping an interim leader pull the school system back together. That meant we needed to keep our own spirits high despite the loss of our leader, friend and confidant. The experience was similar to a death in one's family.

On one especially low day, however, we received a tremendous dose of spirit-lifting medicine. A special education class from a nearby elementary school, accompanied by an enthusiastic teacher's assistant, came to the school district office to sing to us. Those precious young children sang and signed

The Twelve Commandments

the following words from a song by John Mohr and John Mays: "Love in any language, straight from the heart, pulls us all together, never apart and once we learn to speak it, all the world can hear, love in any language fluently spoken here." Those smiling children not only lifted our spirits but gave me, then director of public information, the key to pulling our staff, students and community back together: We simply needed to love each other. If we all worked together, we could accomplish miracles. AND WE DID.

A good illustration of that truth is this story about a traveling saleswoman, a farmer and his old mule, Dooley. It seems that the saleswoman was driving through a rural area in Tennessee on her way to an important business meeting in Nashville. In a hurry to get to the meeting on time, and being unfamiliar with the area, she took a wrong route. While turning her car around, she backed it into a ditch and couldn't get it out. So, she walked to a nearby farmhouse and knocked on the door. An elderly farmer answered her summons.

The saleswoman said, "I've backed my car into a ditch. Would you please get your tractor and pull it out?"

"Ain't got no tractor," the farmer laconically replied.

"Well, I'm in a real bind," the saleswoman persisted. "Is there any way you can help me?"

"Well, I've got a mule," the farmer said after a minute's thought. "He's old and gettin' kinda feeble, but I can hook him up to your car and we'll see what he can do."

The farmer then took a small whip from a hook

on the wall, fetched the mule from the barn, attached a harness with blinders to the mule's head, and led the animal to the saleswoman's car. The farmer hitched the mule to the car with a couple of ropes, cracked the whip once and gruffly ordered, "Pull, Jim!"

Nothing happened.

The farmer cracked his whip again and yelled louder, "Pull, Joe!"

Again, nothing happened.

The third time he cracked the whip, he bellowed, "Pull, Dooley!"

At that, the old mule strained forward, and out came the car.

The saleswoman was thrilled with the result — she was so excited to get her car out of the ditch — but she just had to know why the farmer had approached the problem the way he did.

"Why did you put blinders on the mule so he couldn't see, and why did you first say, 'Pull, Jim,' and then 'Pull, Joe,' before you said, 'Pull, Dooley'?" she asked.

"Well, it's like this," the farmer explained, "Dooley may be old, but he ain't stupid. There ain't no way he was gonna pull that car outta that ditch by hisself."

Therein lies a valuable lesson for all of us. Have you ever thought about how much more successful the business where you work could be if everyone pulled together and worked as a team? I believe the nature of the relationships among the people who work in a business has more to do with the quality and success of that business than any other factor. Team spirit is the winning component.

How do we get this team spirit? Must we all wear blinders? No. I believe we can catch the spirit and spread it with our eyes wide open. Almost everything we accomplish, we must do with and through other people, and that requires us to develop superb interpersonal skills. That successful development begins when we remember to love and respect people.

We need to help our colleagues to see the significant roles they play every day in the duties they perform at work. Every person is flawed, every person makes mistakes, but everyone needs to feel appreciated. This is a most important realization especially for people in management positions because they are responsible for guiding and supporting those in their charge. Every team needs a leader, but the members of every team need and deserve a leader with integrity, compassion and understanding.

Chapter Four
Commandment No. 2: SMILE!

The second commandment is to smile. Practice! Show your teeth. A smile is like a universal language. A smile says, "I am approachable. You can talk to me."

Not long ago, I traveled to Monterrey, Mexico, to speak at a conference of the Association of American Schools of Central America, Colombia, the Caribbean and Mexico. While there, I realized how little Spanish I knew. One morning I tried to order coffee with cream and sugar, but when my order came, I received a cup of black coffee and a box of frosted flakes. So, I drank the coffee and licked the flakes. Even though I could not speak the language of the country, one message came through loud and clear from the people working in the hotel: "We're happy to see you, and we're here to help you." They sent this message with warm smiles, although they could have been snickering at my breakfast choices.

Smiles break down barriers between people, tie us together and enhance open communication, processes vital to teamwork.

I once saw a church sign with this message: "A smile never goes up in price or down in value." Our smiles cost us nothing, but they are invaluable in terms of the messages they send to our families, friends, customers, co-workers and the people we meet as we live in this hectic, busy, complex world.

I remember once meeting a young woman on an escalator in Chicago. She asked me the time. I answered "two o'clock" in my usual unmistakable drawl. She smiled immediately and, in the next breath, said, "I like your Southern accent." It was only a brief encounter, but to a stranger in a town a thousand times bigger than her home, it said, "I like you even if you don't speak the way I do." Her smile added a bright spot to my day.

If you have trouble smiling, try rubbing Vaseline on your teeth. Beauty contestants do this all the time. Think about it: They might not always feel all that great when they're onstage — after all, their swimsuits are stuck to their bodies with hair spray, and duct tape holds up some of their most impressive attributes — but they're always smiling because that is the single most important thing they can do. A smile makes a good first impression, contributing to the recipient's perception of the smiler. People in business have long known the importance of making a good first impression, and that it is quite often the small things that are most important.

Small things certainly impress me. Once William and I checked into a motel in south Georgia. We went to our room and, as is my habit, I immediately headed for the bathroom. There, in that modest motel, was a small strip of paper across the toilet seat. And written on that strip of paper were the words, "For your protection." I wondered what on earth that small strip of paper was supposed to protect me from, but it made a darned good impression. I went ahead and sat down. I just knew everything was going to be okay; I was protected.

Leaving south Georgia, we next drove to the Atlanta area and checked into a larger motel. Again, I headed for the bathroom. This time, there was no comforting strip of paper. I called the front desk and confessed I was worried: "There's no protection in my room. Could you send someone up here to put a band of protection over my toilet seat?"

The desk clerk hung up on me.

I subsequently sat on that toilet with great trepidation, just knowing that some huge hand would reach up and pull me down into the underground sewer system.

Why this story about toilets and strips of paper when I'm trying to stress the importance of smiling? It is to show that even the smallest things, something that costs very little, can make a big difference in people's perceptions. That little strip of paper sends the message that someone has cleaned the toilet and it's okay to use it. A smile sends the message: "I'm a person who likes other people and it's okay to talk to me. You can tell me how you're feeling, pick my brain or give me your opinion. I'm here to help you and I'm interested in you. You are important to me." That's quite a strong message for a simple curving of the mouth. Of course, throwing a little sparkle into the eyes doubles the effect of the smile and tells others, "This is not a fake smile obtained from sleeping with a hanger in my mouth. It's genuine, and just for you."

Facial expression is extremely important in communication. More than 90 percent of what we communicate to our colleagues is through body language, facial expression and tone of voice. We are capable of letting the person next to us know, without saying a word, whether we think that person is doing a good job. We are equally capable, without saying a word, of communicating our disgust or disappointment in that person. If you doubt this, position yourself in front of a mirror the next time you check your child's report card. Then take a good look. You will see what your child sees. You will then know that a message can be sent and received, in total silence; your expression says it all.

Our body language and our facial expressions tell people exactly what we think of them. We can let them know we're proud of them, that we think they've done a good job, or we can say, I'm disgusted with you, I'm disappointed in you. We can send positive and negative messages without uttering a sound and we should remain constantly aware of that ability as we work to promote teamwork.

A smile is such a small thing, but it costs nothing and does quite a lot.

Chapter Five
Commandment No. 3:
Fill The "Buckets" Of Others

The complete third commandment for people who work with people is "Fill The 'Buckets' Of Others. Talk To Them In Such A Way As To Increase Their Self-Esteem." To understand what it means to "fill someone's bucket," you first must understand the opposite, which is to "dip out of someone's bucket." My friend Frankie introduced me to an old Southern expression, "So-and-So dipped out of my bucket." When I asked Frankie to explain the expression to me, she answered, "It means someone took away a little hunk of my self-esteem. He put me down. He rained on my parade."

We all have met bucket-dippers.

I first learned what it meant to have my bucket dipped from when I was in the fifth grade. I had joyfully joined the school chorus and one afternoon, while we were practicing for the spring concert, my music teacher grabbed me by both shoulders and pulled me out of line. "Honey, you can't sing!" she cried. She didn't mean that she wouldn't let me sing but that I *couldn't* sing. I was crushed. I protested that I had already bought the required white dress for the concert! Now, of course, I know that the teacher knew then that the color of my dress would not affect my ability to sing, although I was sure I would sing like a bird in that beautiful white dress. That teacher dipped right out of my bucket — today, I still don't sing or wear white. And that would not be the last time I would suffer such an esteem-lowering experience.

For example, I absolutely love visiting my six-year-old granddaughter, but sometimes she can in her own innocent way dip out of my bucket. Once we were sitting together in the car, waiting for her parents to return from the mall. I remarked to Canaan that pretty soon she would be able to drive and that when I came for a visit, she would be able to drive me around. She looked at me with her big, sweet brown eyes and said, "You'll be dead by then." I protested, "I will not! What makes you think I'll be dead when you get your driver's license?" "Because you're old," she responded. "And just why do you think I'm old?" I asked. She smiled and said, "Because you've got wrinkles." Out of the mouths of babes comes some quite thought-provoking wisdom.

I once read a story in which a seventh grader dipped out of his teacher's bucket. One day, the teacher called on a student named Roger to explain the difference in the meanings of the words "calamity" and "catastrophe." In response, he drawled, "Well, Teacher, I'll tell you, it's like this: If you fell into the river, it would be a 'calamity,' but if the rescue squad got you out, it would be a 'catastrophe'." His words were a tremendous blow to the confidence of his teacher.

People of all ages can dip out of your bucket, even children younger than Roger. For example, one young woman I know told me that she was in the bathroom one day, putting the finishing touches on her makeup under the curious gaze of her visiting four-year-old nephew. After satisfactorily viewing herself in the mirror, she took a bottle of prescription medicine from the cabinet and tapped her "one-tablet-daily" dose into her hand.

Her nephew asked, "What's that for?"

"To make me pretty," she breezily answered.

"Better take two," he innocently, but deadly, responded.

The level in her bucket dipped dramatically.

I was subjected to a similar experience after spending an afternoon in the beauty shop way back in 1966. In those days, women visited the beauty parlor once a week to get their hair "fixed." Getting your hair fixed meant having it washed, rolled on big, bushy wire rollers and sitting under a helmet-style dryer until you were dryer than an over-roasted turkey. After letting you cool off, the beautician would remove the rollers and brush out your hair, leaving you looking pretty good. But she wasn't through. Then it was time to "tease" your hair. Teasing involved back combing every strand of hair on your head, then using a brush to smooth over the top layer of hair until you looked like you were wearing a beehive. One Thursday morning following my usual Wednesday hair-fixing, I was greeted at my classroom door by one of my young female students. She gushed, "Oh, Mrs. White, you look so good! You don't look like yourself!"

She, like many others, had the ability to fill your bucket and empty it, all in the same breath.

Another time, I had lost weight equivalent to 160 sticks of margarine. I had done it by not eating anything that moved or had ever moved; if it had a mother, I didn't eat it. I also had done it by walking. One Sunday afternoon I was out walking when a co-worker passed in her automobile. I waved. The next morning at work, she told me she had seen me. "Oh, Ann, you look great," she complimented. "You've lost so much weight! Your stomach is not nearly as big this week as it was last week!" She, too, had filled my bucket and emptied it, all in the same breath.

The biggest bucket-dipping experience of my life came in November of 1994 when the school system I had served for twenty-five years decided to hire a group of consultants to perform a curriculum study. The hidden agenda of that study had little to do with improving the curricula of the schools. The actual goal was to reduce administrative staff and, thereby, lower costs. It seemed some employees made more money than the School Board thought we should, so the board hired some expensive consultants to show them how they could get along without us, all under the guise of a curriculum study. Those of us who had given most of our lives to the school system felt betrayed. We began to distrust everyone who had any part in the "study" plan. Our team spirit fell to zero.

But there in the midst of it all, I suddenly realized, were the wonderful teachers, library media specialists, other staff members and students with whom I had worked so long — members of the team that I had helped to build and had almost let others erase from my thoughts. I could not let them down by selfishly putting myself and my needs first. Their needs must take precedence. I had to find a way to regain my team spirit, even if the team had to be expanded beyond my immediate co-workers.

When dark times come, it is so easy and tempting for us to focus on a few trees instead of the entire forest. When corporate changes that involve right-sizing, down-sizing, restructuring, performance improvement plans or whatever you want to call them come your way, they can consume big dipperfuls of your self-esteem. Such experiences can cause you to focus on a few trees instead of the entire forest, but you must not allow that to happen; you must always look at the whole forest, the entire team.

How do you do that? First, look beyond any particular tree or trees, *i.e.* obstacle or problems. Look at all the wonderful colleagues who have stood beside you, worked with you and filled your bucket through the years. Look inside yourself, assess your strengths, and realize the tremendous talents you have. Think about the mountains you have already climbed, and fill your own bucket. One of the best ways you can accomplish this is by filling the buckets of others. You will find that when you give others a word of encouragement, a leg-up, a pat on the back when they need it, despite any disappointments of your own, you not only will fill their buckets, but you also will replenish your own.

That said, I have to admit that I have not always followed this commandment. I, too, have been a bucket-dipper, but sometimes seemingly with good cause. For example, I have worked hard to control my weight for more than 30 years, but obviously not hard enough. More than once people have dipped out of my bucket by noticing that I'm not exactly a size twelve ... or a size fourteen either, for that matter. Once I was browsing through racks of clothing in an exclusive ladies' dress shop in Hilton Head, South Carolina, just enjoying looking at the designs and colors when a salesclerk, who looked like she ate pickles three times a day, walked up to me.

"*Honey*, this is the *petite* section," she exclaimed, casting a disparaging eye over my figure.

It was the first time I knew that people my size were not welcome to look at smaller people's clothes.

I looked up at her and innocently inquired, "Where are the dresses in *our* size?"

She had dipped out of my bucket and I reflexively responded, making the mistake of trying to get back at her by taking away a little hunk of her self-esteem. Two people were left smarting from attacks on their appearance. That's what happens when our actions and words diminish the self-image of others. The damage spreads.

It's not worth it.

Chapter Six
Commandment No. 4:
Exhibit A Spirit Of Caring

The fourth commandment is to show people that you care about them. We need to adopt the attitude that everyone is deserving of our respect, attention and assistance. We can begin by dignifying the suggestions of others. Even if you think their suggestions are foolish, you need to look for the good points. It is when people feel that they are in an atmosphere of love and trust and support that they become willing to speak up. They become willing to take risks and offer suggestions because they know they are part of a team, that no one will dip out of their buckets.

Arthur W. Combs, a noted author and educator,

writes in the article, "Perceiving, Behaving and Becoming," for the Association for Supervision and Curriculum Development Journal: "Perhaps the most important single cause of a person's success or failure educationally has to do with the question of what he believes about himself." I believe this is also true regarding a person's success or failure in all areas of life.

I was lucky to have a mother who believed in me, who taught me to love life and people and to laugh at myself even in the worst of circumstances. She faced many struggles and much pain and disappointment in her life, but she never failed to see the humor in every situation and she understood the importance of passing that legacy on to me. When I went to school, many of my teachers stressed the messages that I had talents and I was lovable, even though I was mischievous. They often found themselves laughing at my stories and unsolicited remarks.

But when I was young, I was never much of one to think very far ahead. It was the summer before my senior year in high school that I walked into Stone's Drug Store in Cowpens and asked for a job. I did not know that would be the first step in the most important direction in my life. Dr. Joel Stone hired me to work full time that summer and every afternoon of the following school year. It was from Dr. Stone that I learned some of the most important lessons in life: The customer is always right; hard work never hurt anybody; and laughter is sometimes the best medicine.

For example, as I was working in the pharmacy, I once mused over a prescription that ended with the letters "GYM." Although Dr. Stone had carefully taught me how to read prescriptions, that one stumped me. I consulted him and asked, "What does 'GYM' mean?" Dr. Stone laughed. "Get Your Money," he replied. "Evidently the doctor knows this customer better than we do."

Several months later, Dr. Stone asked if I would like to go to college. I had no immediate answer for him. I simply had never thought about it. After all, I had four older sisters and none of them had gone to college. Going to college would cost money and, in my home, money was always in short supply.

When I hesitated to respond, Dr. Stone told me that if I wanted to go to college, he and his wife, Stella, would send me. I jumped at the chance, and, thanks to that wonderfully caring couple, I entered college and subsequently earned my bachelor's degree. A master's degree and a doctorate would come later, and at my own expense, but those latter achievements would have been unattainable — unthinkable, even — if not for the assistance I received from the Stones.

We can't all send someone else to college, but each of us can extend ourselves to show that we care about the futures of our family, friends, co-workers and neighbors. And if someone has exhibited a strong spirit of caring for you, you can best repay them by passing it on.

We must nurture each other in every facet of our lives, even in the workplace. A good team is like a garden: It must be constantly and carefully nurtured. We do that when we exhibit a spirit of caring and fill the buckets of others.

Keep in mind, however, that your efforts and

words must be sincere. Don't offer compliments as mere lip service. If you look hard, you usually will find more to compliment about your co-workers than the backhanded but strictly truthful words television's Gomer Pyle once offered: "Gee. For a fat girl, you sure don't sweat much." Although he meant well, he certainly dipped out of that girl's bucket.

My husband, William, believes in complimenting women by saying they're cute as a button. It's a habit that annoys me terribly. For one thing, it took me the first fifteen years of our more than thirty-year marriage to figure out what he meant by "as cute as a button." But then one day it dawned on me. There are only three criteria to be as cute as a button in William's eyes: Number One, you have to be female; Number Two, you have to be younger than he is; and, Number Three, smaller than I am. I talk to many audiences full of people who are as cute as a button.

To show caring as a manager or a co-worker, you must be careful in how you nurture the work and spirit of your colleagues. A verbal pat on the back is always acceptable. An offer of assistance or words of encouragement are nearly always appreciated.

One of the worst feelings in the world is that of being unappreciated. I had heard this many times in my life, but never realized how true it was until the school system where I worked ordered the infamous curriculum audit, which, as I've already mentioned, had very little to do with curricula. When my colleagues and I received the results of the audit, which recommended downsizing the administrative staff, we became suspicious of our leaders, rumors were rampant, and trust was destroyed. The team, which had already been damaged by poor, inaccurate communication, fell apart. Several key administrators and some of the system's best teachers ultimately left to seek other career opportunities. The district definitely reached its goal of downsizing, but at a tremendous cost in terms of future employee loyalty, public perception and trust.

During times of restructuring, right-sizing, or downsizing, you should communicate as clearly as possible to your staff about what is happening. Hidden agendas will lead to unrest, unhappiness, distrust and the loss of valuable employees.

The Society for Human Resource Management in a 1997 press release issued the results of a survey regarding employee retention. That survey showed that higher salaries offered by other organizations pose the biggest threat to employee retention, followed by dissatisfaction with potential for career development. Employee perception of not being appreciated (79 percent) was the third leading cause of employees' leaving their jobs. Also among the top six reasons was conflicts with supervisors or coworkers (62 percent).

Good pay, career development opportunities and fair treatment are key initiatives for keeping good employees. Employers who show their staffs that they care about them by providing health care benefits, orientation and training programs, an open communications policy, competitive salaries and retirement programs will have little trouble in keeping a positive, goal-oriented team. For extra measure, employers might want to throw in some goodies such as early-leave passes, on-site parking, a fitness center for employee use, casual-dress programs, child care facilities and some team socials. These items all send the message, "WE CARE ABOUT YOU."

Chapter Seven
Commandment No. 5:
Display A "Can Do" Attitude

I believe the world is tilted in favor of people who believe that something can be done about any problem. You can have years of education, an abundance of specialized training, and a high IQ, but all of that can prove useful or useless, depending upon your attitude. Once I was reviewing applications for the position of school secretary. On the application was the question, "Why did you leave your last job?" One applicant wrote, "Because my boss gave me a bad attitude." Apparently she had missed out on the good news about attitude, which is that you are in charge of it. You can get up in the morning and decide what kind of day you are going to have. You can choose to be confident instead of frustrated, competent instead of clumsy. You can opt every day to have a positive, cheerful, expectant attitude, realizing that other people can negatively affect your attitude only to the extent that you allow them to do so. You are the one in charge.

So, go ahead. Get up in the morning, look in the mirror and, while you're putting Vaseline on your teeth, have a little talk with yourself. Say, "Today, I'm going to have a great day! It's going to be a wonderful day. Nothing is going to happen today that the good Lord and I together can't handle."

You must beware of the "I'll never be able to do it" syndrome, in which afflicted people can be heard uttering such phrases as, "Nobody likes me," "I'm just a nobody," "I'm ugly," "I can't do anything right." Such people dip out of their own buckets and will empty yours if you're not careful. They tend to try to tell you why you can't hope to accomplish the tasks or goals you have set for yourself. Even though they may realistically paint a picture of ice on your path or roadblocks in your way, you must allow yourself the right to slip, to stumble, even to fall, but you must always have the strength to bounce back up again. Remember the goal-setter's creed, taken from the book, *The Secrets of Goal-Setting*, by Dan Zadra: "I give myself the right to make mistakes. I treat all setbacks as temporary. It's not what happens to me that counts, but how I handle it. It's not how far I fall that really matters, but how high I bounce."

I once read a story that reveals the epitome in self-confidence. It seems a kindergarten student was painting a subject that her teacher couldn't quite identify. So the teacher asked, "What are you painting?" The child responded, "I'm painting a picture of God." The little boy next to her said, "But no one knows what God looks like." The little girl confidently assured, "THEY WILL NOW!"

Choose to be positive. Expect the best. Surround yourself with positive, inspirational people who will tell you why you can, why you want to, and why you will succeed in your endeavors. Envision yourself as a winner, achieving your goals. Then, on the way to work, play or sing uplifting music. When you go into the workplace, smiling and feeling positive, you will find that others will reflect your attitude. Other members of your team, by reacting to your positive attitude, will help to engender a positive atmosphere for all.

Remember, though, that you must do everything you can to adjust your attitude for the day, and that just might include singing that uplifting song I mentioned, on your way to work. Now you may recall that I don't sing, but there is a song I would like to recommend for you to sing on your way to work or any time you need to build or rebuild your own spirit. It's "Zip-A-Dee-Do-Dah." Even if you were kicked out of the school chorus, try singing this song, and metaphorically get others to join you.

Almost anyone will sing if other people sing beside them. Even I, who my music teacher said couldn't, will sing if others stand beside me and help me. What about the people in your business? Do they need a team member who will stand beside them and help them sing? Do they need someone who has the attitude that we're in this together, and together we can succeed? If you go into work singing that uplifting song, others around you will begin to sing it, too. It's infectious.

If you don't think you and your co-workers constitute a choir, think again. If team members have others standing beside them, helping them, they will feel better about doing tasks they ordinarily would not feel competent to tackle. They will go through any day with a smile, even if it starts with a dead cat at their feet.

Chapter Eight
Commandment No. 6:
Beware! The "Chicken Little Syndrome" Is Contagious

Do you remember the story of Chicken Little, who was standing in the barnyard one day when an acorn fell from a tree and hit her on the head? That little fowl did not take time to analyze the situation but jumped to the first obvious, though incorrect, conclusion: The sky was falling. She rushed to tell her friends, most of whom accepted the story as truth, and they helped to spread the word. Because of a personal misinterpretation of an isolated incident, Chicken Little disseminated a mistaken story of doom and gloom. And her whole team accepted it as truth.

Too many people in the workplace are prone to shout, "The sky is falling, the sky is falling!" every time they see a dead cat on their desk. Henny Penny, Goosey Lucy, Ducky Lucky, Turkey Lurky, all are waiting in your workplace, ready to follow your lead. There are people in every barnyard ready to be afflicted with the Chicken Little Syndrome, and they can destroy your can-do attitude.

To guard against that happening, you must separate your attitude from that person with the Chicken Little Syndrome. You have to say you prefer to be positive, you prefer to see the glass half full instead of half empty.

How do you recognize people with the Chicken Little Syndrome? Listen. Their conversations will include such phrases as "It won't work here," "We've never done it that way before," "We tried that once, but it didn't work," "Let's stick to what we know."

You have to remember, and to remind them, that if you always do what you've always done, you'll always get what you've always gotten, and sometimes that isn't good enough. Progress would not exist without someone taking risks, trying to accomplish a task in a new and better way, and it may be up to you to provide the inspiration.

Consider these words from Gandhi:

"Keep my words positive;
My words become my behavior.
Keep my behavior positive;
My behavior becomes my habits.
Keep my habits positive;
My habits become my values.
Keep my values positive;
My values become my destiny."

Sometimes the Chicken Little Syndrome may masquerade behind the "It's not my job" mask. It's easy to dampen team spirit by refusing to become involved in a task that is not included in your job description.

I know one school principal who regularly helps serve soft drinks and hot dogs at gatherings for parents. It's not in her job description, but just think how it inspires others because she is willing to do it, and do it with a smile. Because parents see that this dedicated principal is willing to go above and beyond her stated duties, they become more willing to get involved in school projects, and that is why support for this school has grown in its community. Sometimes we have to go outside our spheres of expertise and attempt extra duties to gain cooperation from the people we want on our team.

And sometimes the effort proves difficult. A friend who worked at a daily newspaper once told me how, in the years before computers turned writers and editors into compositors, the composing room (the department where editorial and advertising copy used to be assembled, pages laid out, and the newspaper readied for printing) had one rule guaranteed to destroy any possibility of team spirit among departments. The rule was: Follow copy, even if it jumps out the window. That meant that if a composing room employee spotted an error anywhere, in an article or an advertisement, he or she was to ignore it because it wasn't his or her job to point it out. The thinking was, "It's not my job, so it's not my fault."

But the newspaper's readers didn't know whose fault anything was, so they blamed the entire staff for mistakes. It took years before that particular newspaper overcame the "it's not my job" attitude and worked on engendering team spirit among all departments. In the process, they produced a generally better product.

We have to remember that mistakes affect the whole team, not just the person who makes them. Everybody needs to adopt the attitude, "It *is* my job. We are *all* in this together, and *together* we will succeed or fail." Because that is the truth.

To help your team avoid the Chicken Little Syndrome, you may want to follow these suggestions:

Give praise for a job well done. Delight in the efforts of your superiors, co-workers and subordinates and try to be specific with your comments. Say, "I like the way you organized your thoughts in this report because it helps me understand the problem better," or, "I really admire the way you handled that customer's complaint in such a positive manner that she walked away with a smile."

Give constant feedback. Everyone likes to know how he or she is doing. If you don't believe that, try going on a diet and see how often you weigh yourself.

Choose your words carefully when you communicate with your colleagues. Be sure to use exactly the words you need to convey the message you mean, because sometimes a seemingly insignificant comment may cause someone to beam with pride or frown with disappointment.

Pay attention to the tone of your voice and to your body language. People may forget what you say, but they will never forget how you delivered the message and how that delivery made them feel.

Talk *with* people, not *at* them. Avoid terms that belittle, humiliate or embarrass. Always focus on the positive as much as possible when communicating. Say, "I have faith in you," not "you'll probably find this difficult." Negative words have a negative impact; the converse is also true.

Dignify the responses of others. Nothing can destroy teamwork quicker than ignoring or belittling someone's suggestions.

Never forget that criticism crushes. Delivering constructive criticism is an art because nearly everyone tends to take all criticism negatively. Negative criticism destroys self-confidence, trust and respect. To inspire, you must be a careful and caring critic who is willing to offer suggestions and possible solutions to problems at the same time you point them out.

Set high expectations. People usually try to live up to what you expect from them. Of course, it is important to be realistic regarding the standards you set: It is unfair to expect performance beyond a person's understanding and/or ability.

Empathize. Put yourself in the other person's place, to see how your words or actions might affect that person.

Work as a team. As you work, show confidence in other team members, especially when someone makes a mistake. Admit your own mistakes. Colleagues will appreciate knowing that you don't think you are perfect.

Solicit input. Let colleagues help make decisions insofar as is possible and practical. Think how good it makes you feel when someone asks for your ideas.

Show genuine concern. Most people can spot phoniness in a second. Be sincere.

Listen. Listening, more than almost anything else you can do, shows that you care about others. Listening sends the message, "You are important."

Respect individuality. Don't compare one person's work to that of another. People have different talents, capabilities and personalities. If every team member had the same talents, no one would be challenged to excel and little of merit could be accomplished.

Encourage pride and responsibility by delegating authority. When a person is given responsibility, it increases the person's feelings of self-worth and capability.

Boost self-esteem by displaying the work of others. Posting a report or an exceptional graphic for all to see shows that you are proud of the work someone has done and think it is worth sharing.

Make good news public. Including congratulatory messages in an organization's newsletter or interoffice memo is great public relations.

Help others set and achieve goals. Nothing boosts self-esteem like the satisfaction that comes with successfully achieving a goal. And remember that these goals may be ones you help supervisors set for the entire organization, ones you set for yourself, or ones that you assist others to set for themselves.

Encourage organization-wide recognition programs. These may be as all-encompassing as an annual banquet to recognize employees' contributions or as informal as a thank-you notice on a workspace bulletin board. Be sure to recognize achievements in all areas and on all levels of the organization.

Think positive. We've been over this before but I can't say it often enough: Positive thoughts encourage positive actions; negative, likewise.

Provide enriching experiences. Work should not be boring. Whenever possible, give team members choices in their tasks, and enable them to have as much fun as possible along the way.

Keep a sense of humor. It's a proven fact: Laughter reduces tension and stress. It improves camaraderie. Laughter can even boost self-confidence.

Need I say more?

Chapter Nine
Commandment No. 7:
Strive For Quality In All You Do

Communication is one of the areas in which we must strive for quality if we are to achieve a team spirit in our workplace. Trickle-down (incomplete or unclear) communication leads to confusion and misunderstandings, to rumors, gossip and distrust — it destroys teamwork. We must become quality communicators, and, to do that, we must remember the four "C's." Communication should be Concise, Clear, Correct and Complete. Leaders may have superior skills, a wealth of knowledge, and expertise in their fields, and still not be successful. Why? Because of their inability to communicate effectively.

I used to have a supervisor who would give me

only one little piece of the puzzle and expect me to
acquire the rest of what I needed to solve it. I wasted
more time going to fellow team members to try to
get other pieces of the puzzle than I spent doing my
job!

If you have a problem that needs to be solved,
enlist the whole team. But be sure you communicate
the problem in its entirety. Give the team all the
pieces they need of the puzzle. Don't let your co-
workers waste time because they don't have those
pieces. Then provide specific feedback. Specific
knowledge of results is an important factor for moti-
vation. When such feedback is not provided, people
may feel that they are working in a vacuum, unsure
whether they are making headway, whether the
team is achieving its goals.

I have found that there are four primary steps to
quality in the workplace. First, do your job; second,
do a good job; third, help others do a good job; and
fourth, tell others about the good job you and your
team are doing.

There will be times that you will fail, times that
you will suffer embarrassment. I'll never forget the
first talent show in which I performed. I was a sixth-
grader at Clifton Elementary School and had received a toy plastic clarinet for Christmas. I thought
I was really good at playing "Twinkle, Twinkle,
Little Star," on that little piece of plastic and it
never occurred to me to question how others might
perceive such a performance. The day of the contest,
I was confidently blowing into that clarinet, sure I
was doing a wonderful job. I had gotten as far as
"Like a diamond in the sky," when I provoked a
noise that sounded a lot like a snake trying to swal-

low a dog. The toy horn had broken. I was mortified by the giggles from the audience and ran off stage. My friends teased me about it for weeks.

But we all have such moments in our lives. The important thing is not to get down on yourself after such an embarrassment, not to say, "How could I ever be so stupid? What a dumb mistake! I must be an idiot! I always goof!" Okay, you're allowed to say it once or twice, but then you must forget it and move on. Playing mistakes over and over in your mind is a bad habit that will make you miserable and keep you from progressing. I could have let that one embarrassing incident in my youth keep me from ever performing before an audience again, but I did not. Instead, I let memories of that humiliation provide a source of empathy for others who find themselves in similar situations, and I tell them that they, too, can overcome any failure. If I had known then what I know now, I never would have asked for that toy clarinet for Christmas.

Today I am familiar with Dr. Howard Gardner's Theory of Multiple Intelligences. Dr. Gardner, a Harvard University psychologist, identified through his research the following intelligences: linguistic, logical-mathematical, bodily-kinesthetic, spatial, musical, interpersonal and intrapersonal. According to Dr. Gardner, we all have some of each of these intelligences, but we are stronger in some forms than in others. Obviously, musical intelligence was not one of my strengths. While my teachers at that time did not have access to Dr. Gardner's research, they still understood that students' talents are in different areas. My teachers helped me to understand that, while I was not a musician, I was still a capable and competent person, and they steered me to other areas of opportunity.

You know, a lot of people refer to animals as dumb, but some animals seem to be a lot smarter than humans when it comes to recovering from mistakes. I once read a story about a small group of squirrels scurrying around, collecting chestnuts. As they worked, one little fellow picked up a small stone by mistake. As soon as it was in his mouth, however, he realized his error. He simply spat it out and happily went back to the business of collecting more chestnuts. The other squirrels didn't laugh, they didn't make a big deal out of it. And, most important, that little squirrel didn't let his mistaken judgment ruin his day. If we don't expect a dumb squirrel to sit around and worry about how he could ever have mistaken a common stone for a chestnut and fret about what the other squirrels must think about him, why do we allow ourselves to do it to ourselves? We must learn to accept our mistakes and go on about our business, resolving firmly to do better in the future.

We all could learn from the story of a grocery store clerk working in the produce department. On one particularly harried day, this clerk was confronted with a customer who wanted to buy a half head of lettuce. The clerk patiently explained to the customer that the store did not sell half heads of lettuce. The customer was insistent, so the clerk continued to explain. He said, "Sir, we've already weighed, wrapped and priced this lettuce. I simply cannot sell you a half head." This still did not satisfy the customer, so the clerk walked to the back of the store to consult his manager. The frustrated clerk said, "There's some fool out here who would like to buy a half head of lettuce." To his dismay, he then discovered that the customer had followed him and was standing right behind him. Thinking fast, he added, "And this nice gentlemen here would like to buy the other half." It's easy to put our foot into our mouth and come out with statements that hurt others, damage teamwork and land us in a jam.

Regardless of what happens, you must never lose confidence in yourself. Even in your worst hours, you must realize that your resources are far greater and deeper than you might have imagined. When you encounter unexpected situations (dead cats), you should never ask, "*Will* I survive this?" but "*How* can I recover and continue my quest for quality?" The answer is there. If you expect it to come to you, it will.

In our efforts to achieve quality, we will make mistakes. The important thing is to learn from these past experiences. If we don't learn from these incidents, we are what someone has called "insane." According to this person, insanity is when we do the same things over and over again, expecting to get different results. For example, some of us keep expecting to get thin, yet we continue to overeat.

Our mistakes should help us develop savvy. As a young teacher, I made mistakes that helped me become a better teacher. I remember once, while I was on recess duty, Susie, one of my eighth-grade students, came to me to tell me that her mother had arrived early to pick her up. Since I was on duty, I did not go into the school to verify that it was indeed her mother who had come for her. I simply gave her permission to leave. After recess, I returned to class and learned from another student that Susie had left with her boyfriend, not her mother. And to make matters worse, the informer said, "I think they are running away to get married." I immediately had visions of losing my teacher's certification and of being sued for all I was worth. Fortunately, Susie did not get married, and she had an understanding mother who did not make an issue of my mistake. You can bet that I never did that again.

Later, when I became a school librarian, I worked in a library located in a portable classroom outside the main building. One day I was telling a story to a group of first graders seated on the floor. One little fellow, Tony, could not be quiet or still for my story. So, I took him by the hand and led him to my workroom in the back, leaving him with explicit directions not to come out until I said he could. I finished my story, took the other children back into the main building, talked to the teacher, ate my lunch, and then returned to the library. Once inside, I realized that Tony was still in the workroom; I had never told him to come out. I ran into the back, did some major sucking up to Tony and gently took him back to his classroom. That could have been a career-defining moment for me — it could have cost me my job. Instead, I learned a valuable lesson from the incident and, believe it or not, I became a successful educator.

Quality does not come easily, but little in life does. Achieving quality depends largely on our ability to learn from our mistakes, to set appropriate goals, and to get others to support those goals. People will usually support ideas and programs that they have had a part in developing. Our goals should be appropriate, specific, achievable, measurable and congruent with our abilities.

Chapter Ten
Commandment No. 8:
Help People More;
Hassle People Less

In many areas, life has become more difficult than it needs to be. I am convinced that every organization needs to examine all its rules, regulations and policies. We need to question whether those rules, regulations and policies help the people in the organizations do their jobs, or whether they just hassle people.

Imagine what would happen if a company actually adopted a restroom-use policy like this one:

"At the beginning of each month, every employee will receive 20 restroom credits, which cannot be accumulated from month to month. The credits will be redeemed by the use of a voice-print- recognition device as each employee speaks before entering the bathroom. Of course, the installation and use of this voice recognition tool will require a considerable investment of time and money on the part of the company but it will prove well worth it by reducing excessive time spent by employees in the bathroom."

"Before the program begins, each employee will be required to give management two copies of his or her voice print, one in the employee's regular speaking voice, the other under stress [think about it]. If an employee's restroom credits reach zero before the end of the month, the door to all company bathrooms will not open for that person's voice until the beginning of the next month. Additionally, all company bathrooms will be equipped with timed toilet paper retractors. At the end of three minutes, the toilet paper will retract, the commode will flush, the door will fly open and the hapless employee's picture will be taken with a hidden camera. The result will be added to the employee's personnel file, or posted on the company bulletin board."

That would be quite a portrait, wouldn't it, of a company going off the deep end in an effort to control and improve employees' use and abuse of personal privileges. If such a policy were adopted, the company most likely would spend more money setting up and maintaining the program than the employees would have wasted through misspent time.

But stranger things have actually happened that make you wonder if hassling people has been elevated to an art. For example, after browsing through a local gift shop, I selected an item for purchase from the sale table. As I paid for the item, I asked if I could get it gift wrapped. After all, a prominently displayed sign advertised free gift wrapping for purchases.

"I'm sorry," the clerk replied, "but we don't gift wrap items that are on sale."

"Okay," I said. "I'll be happy to pay you to gift wrap it."

"Sorry. We don't gift wrap items on sale even if you pay for the wrapping" was the nonsensical response.

One of my favorite places to shop is the home accessories department of a large discount department store chain. Unfortunately, there is something that ticks me off (that means the same as "makes me angry") when I visit some of these stores. Many of the chain's facilities here in the Southeast keep their bathroom doors locked. If you need to use the bathroom, you must find a clerk and have her unlock the door for you. It's ridiculous and demeaning. Once, one of the employees in the layaway department became upset with me when I asked her to unlock the bathroom door. She barked, "Who told you to come to me?" Like a reprimanded child, I said, "My friend that I am shopping with said this was the place to come." "Well, it's not," she said. "You'll have to go to the front register." I told her then and there that I intended to include the incident in this book under the commandment, "Help People More, Hassle People Less." Then I went to the front where I found a woman with a nametag reading, "Third Key Operator," who unlocked the door for me. Do you suppose that three people actually have the key to the bathroom? Is there a first and second key operator? Is that their only job?

Most people will tell you that government agencies from the federal Internal Revenue Service to any state's Department of Motor Vehicles are noted for their ability to hassle people. My most recent experience resulted from my attempt to obtain a passport. In completing the process, I learned that my birth certificate was unacceptable because it was a "delayed birth certificate" — delayed in that I had never received a copy until I was thirty-five years old. I had spent many hours preparing and gathering the documentation to get the birth certificate. Now, the passport police wanted me to send them the same documentation that I had worked so hard to gather for the Department of Vital Statistics for the State of South Carolina fifteen years earlier.

After I finally assembled the requested documentation in its entirety and mailed it off, I had to wait several more weeks for a response. And then what I received wasn't my passport but a letter instructing me to have an enclosed affidavit signed by someone who would swear to know about my birth and that I was a United States citizen. That completed, I had to wait again on the lengthy processing of the mail.

Hassle. Unnecessary hassle.

And the practice extends to all areas of our lives. As the mother of three children who were educated in the public schools, I recall those children coming home from their first day of school every August with stacks of papers for me to sign. They greeted me individually as I came in the door from work on those days, each dumping a sheaf of printed forms into my lap and warning, "Mama, you have to sign all these papers for me before I can go back to school tomorrow." What! The paper police would individually inspect each child's bookbag and prevent his entering the classroom if each and every paper wasn't signed? Well, like most parents, I didn't want to take that chance, so I got out my pen and flexed my fingers. It takes more paperwork to get a child back in school the second day than it does to get married or divorced!

Following the completion of all those forms, invariably one of my children would say, "Mama, I need four composition books before tomorrow — one red, one yellow, one green and one blue." That meant I had to drive to the nearest Kmart, which was eight miles away, praying that it would still be open and that the four required colors in composition books would be in stock.

One year our daughter Lori had a Clemson University graduate for a teacher. Being a true blue (or should I say a true orange?) fan of the university, he wanted Lori to have an orange composition book for his class. I don't know about where you live, but in our small town, an orange composition book is almost impossible to find. I think I drove 15 miles to find that one.

But, after knocking people out of the way and grabbing the right colors of composition books for so many years, I am convinced that this requirement works. All three of my children were graduated from high school and college, and I am certain it is because they always had the right colors of composition books. I can't imagine how they might have turned out if I had not been willing to drive that occasional eight extra miles.

On the opposite side of the coin, however, some

folks really have their act together when it comes to helping. For example, after a recent flight to Vancouver, I was standing at the airport baggage claim, patiently waiting for my bags to roll out, when a Delta agent approached me and asked, "Are you Ann White?"

"Yes, I am."

"I'm sorry," she said, "but one of your bags was mistakenly sent to Los Angeles, and it will be about an hour before it arrives here in Vancouver."

She knew my bag was missing even before I did and ensured that I would not have to stand in lines to inquire about what procedures to follow. She sought me out to save me time, worry and lost energy. She made the mistake her problem, not mine, and assured me that it would be rectified with the least inconvenience to me. I will fly Delta every chance I get.

Accolades also go to the staff of Dutch Fork High School in South Carolina. After a speaking engagement there, I discovered that one of a treasured pair of my angel earrings was missing. The earrings had been a Christmas gift from my husband, William, who had enclosed a note reading, "I thought these would be perfect for you since you're always up in the air about something and continually harping about something and you never have a heavenly thing to wear."

Distraught at my loss, I called a secretary at the school who enlisted the help of other secretaries, administrators and maintenance staffers to search for the missing earring.

That secretary could have said, "I'm so sorry, but I don't have time to help you." Her fellow secretaries could have agreed.

Those administrators could have said, "It's not our job," and they would have been right. I'm pretty sure searching for lost earrings is not in their job description.

And the maintenance personnel could have said, "It was probably swept out in the trash; it would be like looking for a needle in a haystack. Sorry."

But they didn't. They searched high and low until they found that tiny earring and returned it, rendering me ever grateful to them and eternally securing a warm place in my heart for anybody even remotely connected with Dutch Fork High School.

Everybody likes being helped and nobody likes being hassled. Before we think of instituting policies and procedures for anything, we need to measure the hassle factor to make sure the outcome will be worth it and to consider its effect on teamwork.

Chapter Eleven
Commandment No. 9:
Never Be Afraid To Try To
Make Things Better

Just think about what a difference it would make in your business if every member of your team dared to try to make things better. A wiser person than I said, "If you always do what you've always done, you'll always get what you've always gotten, or less." For that reason, we should never be afraid to try to make things better. Even if we fail, we will have shown that we cared enough to try to make a difference.

A devoted football fan of my acquaintance took umbrage at remarks made in a press conference b- then Carolina Panthers Coach Dom Capers. C paring the winning season the NFL team had had two years earlier with its dismal 0-4 start (and it did get much, much worse) in 1998, Capers commented, "I don't know what's wrong. We're still doing what we were doing two years ago. I'm still exactly the coach I was two years ago."

The disgusted fan shouted at the television screen, "Well, you dummy, that's what's wrong! You're not doing anything different, and everybody else is!" Eventually, Capers was replaced as head coach, and the National Football League team's game plan was rethought and retooled.

As you've already read, football is not my game and I haven't a clue as to the truth of what needed to be done to transform the Panthers into a winning team. But I suspect that fan was right. Change in your life is not only inevitable, it is necessary just to stay even. Change, if carefully considered, can be good and improve our lives. I am thankful things change; else, I would still be wearing hosiery requiring a garter belt. I am eternally grateful to the person who invented pantyhose.

Most of us have heard the adage, "Build a better mousetrap and the world will beat a path to your door," but too many people ignore the advice. Numerous companies have suffered financial distress, even bankruptcy, in recent years because they failed to keep abreast of trends and changes in the marketplace. What happened to all the companies that made typewriters? What about the Beta VCR's? Zippers replaced buttons which replaced hooks which replaced strings; and Velcro has zipper-makers looking over their shoulders. Numerous products have been invented over the years to serve exactly the same purpose, and those who failed to note the changes in the market place lived to regret it. But to some, change is anathema.

Here, in our small town of Cowpens, we have one traffic light. Several years ago, town officials, working with the State Department of Transportation, decided to install another traffic light. But area residents and travelers through the town complained so much about the second light that it was removed.

Even once-promising cities have failed to grow into major markets because of fear of change. A friend who is a long-time resident of a large but conservative Southern city blames that city's failure to keep pace with modern Atlanta on the attitude of the vocal majority of its populace. In fact, she says her city's prevailing attitude toward progress is poignantly illustrated by this riddle: How many people does it take to change a light bulb in my hometown? Answer: Three. One to screw in the new bulb and two to sit around and talk about how good the old bulb used to be.

The plaint, "We've never done it that way before," should be considered a challenge to try to make things better.

But making things better can extend into the personal arena, too. One supervisor at a medium-size company noticed that one of her staff members had begun reporting to work late in the mornings, leaving early in the afternoons, and usually could be found at night in a local bar. She knew his wife had recently died unexpectedly, that all his children were married and busy with families of their own, and she suspected that he was suffering from deer depression compounded by growing alcoholism. A little circumspect investigation and a couple of heart-to-heart talks with this staff member who was old enough to be her father confirmed her suspicions. So, she determined to try to help him: She called one of his daughters, met with her, explained her concerns and, together, they approached the troubled man. Although he initially denied the validity of any reason for their concern, he later agreed to seek counseling through the company's confidential employee-assistance program. The supervisor worked with the company's benefits department to help the employee obtain a partially-paid medical leave of absence which allowed him to enter an alcohol rehabilitation program. Thanks to the help initiated by his supervisor, this employee eventually excelled again in the performance of his duties, and his family, acknowledging his problems, rallied more closely around him.

That supervisor could have merely written the employee up for excessive tardiness and absences; instead, she showed compassion and understanding coupled with a resolve to make things better for that employee, personally and professionally. She took a chance that his family would respond favorably to her overtures and that the employee himself would take the offered opportunity to change his life. Her effort to make things better cost her nothing but time, and that investment was repaid royally.

It took the serious illness of one of my children for me to realize I could make my life better. For years, I had let my work as a school administrator consume my life. Often, I worked seven days a week, leaving little time for my family and other areas of

The Twelve Commandments

my life. During the illness of my child, however, I re-examined my life; I traveled on the road less traveled. With the help of a good counselor who helped me understand that we always have choices, I was able to improve my life immensely and to see the importance of achieving balance in my life. "Making things better" often requires us to examine and scrutinize our choices. Og Mandino in his book, *The Greatest Miracle in the World*, writes: "We have the power to choose. Choose to:

"Love rather than hate."

"Laugh rather than cry."

"Create rather than destroy."

"Persevere rather than quit."

"Praise rather than gossip."

"Heal rather than wound."

"Give rather than steal."

"Act rather than procrastinate."

"Grow rather than rot."

"Pray rather than curse."

"Live rather than die."

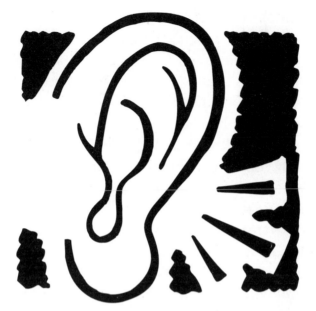

Chapter Twelve
Commandment No. 10:
<u>Train</u> Your Ears
And <u>Tame</u> Your Tongue

This probably is the most difficult command-ment on this list, or at least it is for me. Training your ears and taming your tongue is so difficult, especially for an assertive person. I like to talk, and what I really have to guard against when I'm work-ing with a team is not to take over the team. No one person should ever rule the team. There are a lot of people who are less assertive than I am and I need to shut my mouth and give them an opportunity to open theirs. I believe those people who are less as-sertive will speak up if some of us who are more assertive will shut up and let them talk.

A number of large companies recently have advocated the practice of "active listening" for managers in their dealings with the people they supervise. The idea is that sometimes an attentive audience is all that people want; if an employee feels that a complaint has been heard and understood, the employee will be satisfied. To that end, managers are instructed in role-playing and in keeping their cool even if complaints are aimed personally at them or their managerial styles. The object is for the manager to impart the message, "What you have to say is important; I am listening; I understand; I will consider your words and take the appropriate action." And, believe me, it takes a lot of practice to be able to listen to complaints and respond only with, "Let me repeat what you have said to be sure I understand it." Of course, managers then are expected to follow through on complaints and to do their best to resolve them. But the first and most important step is to have dealt successfully with the employee by listening to what the employee has to say.

Robert W. Bly, president of the Center for Technical Education in Dumont, New Jersey, writes that most people are not good listeners. Bly cites a survey conducted by Sperry Corporation, a company that has built its corporate identity around the theme of good listening, as noting that 85 percent of all people questioned rated themselves average or less in listening abilities. Fewer than 5 percent rated themselves either superior or excellent. Bly writes that you can come up with a pretty good idea of where you fall in this spectrum by thinking about your relationships with the people in your life — your boss, colleagues, subordinates, best friend or spouse.

If asked, what would they say about how well you listen? Do you often misunderstand assignments, or only vaguely remember what people have said to you? If so, you may need to improve your listening skills.

My husband always says I am not a good listener, and that is based totally on one incident. One afternoon, William and I were in the grocery store in Cowpens, trying to find something for supper. We both had meetings that night and we were rushing up and down the aisles, trying to get something quick and easy to prepare.

Suddenly William stopped me and said, "Ann, I really need to tell you something."

I brushed him off. "William, let it wait. We'll be home soon."

I hurriedly pushed the cart up another aisle but he followed.

"Ann," he insisted, "I really need to tell you something."

"William, please! Just let it wait."

He swelled up in a pout and didn't speak to me again until after we got home. We had carried the groceries inside the house and had put them away before he finally turned to me and asked, "Can I tell you something now?"

"Go ahead," I said with a sigh.

"Well, for the last hour, I've been trying to tell you that the bottom of your skirt is tucked up in the top of your pantyhose."

Let me tell you that I listen to the old boy now whenever he opens his mouth. I quickly learned that it pays to listen if you don't want to show your behind.

In a more learned vein, Stephen Covey in his book, *Seven Habits of Highly Effective People*, puts it like this: "Seek first to understand, then to be understood." In the vernacular, that translates: Shut up and listen, be sure you understand what you have just heard, that you have all the details and the other person is through expressing himself, then think about what you want to say, and, finally, talk. We all should endeavor to keep that advice in the forefront of our minds as we deal with team members in the workplace.

The following tips can help you become a better listener:

Give your full attention to the person who is talking. Put other things that are happening around you out of your mind. This shows you care about what the person is saying.

Don't lose your focus. Don't jump ahead to thinking about how you will respond before the speaker has finished.

Show the speaker that you understand what he or she is saying. Do this by repeating what the speaker has said to let him or her know that you have received and understood the message.

Stifle any desire you have to interrupt. Any question you may have may be answered in the speaker's next sentence.

Listen with your eyes as well as your ears. Observe the body language of the speaker. This should help you gain a clearer understanding of what he or she is saying.

Sometimes we are guilty of only partially listening and making our own assumptions about what a person is trying to say. I am reminded of the story of a kindergarten teacher who was helping a student put on her boots. The teacher tugged and tugged to get the boots on the little girl. Finally, when she had them on the child, the little girl looked up at her and said, "These aren't my boots." The teacher pulled and pulled until she finally removed the boots, only to hear the youngster add, "They're my brother's boots, but my mother made me wear them." The teacher had made a mistake, and cost herself more work, by jumping ahead of the speaker.

I also try, whenever possible, to remember HALT. This acronym reminds me to try not to make decisions or speak without appropriate consideration whenever I am: Hungry, Angry, Lonely or Tired. Under HALT conditions, it is easy to misread or overreact to situations. Waiting one day, or taking time to cool off, may make a positive difference. Sometimes we need to put skid chains on our thoughts as well as our tongues.

The Twelve Commandments

Chapter Thirteen
Commandment No. 11:
Tell The Truth.
It's A Lot Easier To Remember.

Sir Walter Scott said it best: "O what a tangled web we weave, when first we practice to deceive." What he didn't explain was that we usually get trapped in our own webs and ultimately pay the price for lying.

I have to tell a story of which I am ashamed. When I was fifteen years old, I got my driver's license, and almost the first thing my mother said to me was, "Don't drive anybody else's car." Well, I hadn't even thought about that until she mentioned it, which should raise a caution flag for those of you who have aspiring teenage drivers. But I had this boyfriend whom, for the sake of protecting his identity (although I don't think his mother would ground him at this late stage of the game), I will call Tom, and Tom had a "new" used car. One night I talked Tom into letting me drive his new used car. I drove south on Highway 29 into Spartanburg and turned left on Connecticut Avenue in front of the entrance to prestigious Converse College. As I approached the intersection of Connecticut Avenue and Otis Boulevard, I failed to see the stop sign on Connecticut Avenue. I whipped right past it. And a car traveling north on Otis Boulevard hit us on Tom's side, for which I selfishly thanked the Lord. Tom's door flew open and, this being in the days before seat belts were invented, much less required, he fell into the street.

Now let me remind you I was only fifteen.

I immediately jumped from the driver's side and went over to where Tom was lying in the street. Did I ask him if he was hurt? No. Did I ask him if he was in pain? No. Did I ask him if he was alive? No. Knowing that the police would soon arrive to investigate the accident in this posh neighborhood, what I said was, "Tom, get up and tell them *you* were driving."

In some excessive spirit of chivalry, or maybe it was stupidity, he did. As a result, he lost his driver's license. (But he should have. After all, he had run a stop sign.)

I lost Tom.

Credibility once lost is almost impossible to regain. Credibility is crucial and should be coveted.

The images and reputations of two United States Presidents have been tarnished forever because of their failure to tell the truth. Richard Milhouse Nixon, the 37th President, achieved much while in office. His accomplishments while in the nation's highest office included revenue sharing, the end of the draft, new anti-crime laws and a broad environmental program. As he had promised, Nixon appointed justices of conservative philosophy to the Supreme Court. Some of his most acclaimed achievements came in his quest for world stability. During visits in 1972 to Beijing and Moscow, he reduced tensions with China and the Soviet Union. His summit meetings with Russian leader Leonid I. Brezhnev produced a treaty to limit strategic nuclear weapons. In January 1973, Nixon announced an accord with North Vietnam to end American involvement in Indochina.

But will Nixon be remembered for these accomplishments? Unfortunately, no! He will be remembered for his part in the so-called "Watergate" scandal, stemming from a break-in at the offices of the Democratic National Committee during the 1972 campaign. The break-in was traced to officials of the Committee to Re-elect the President. A number of Nixon administration officials resigned; some were later convicted of offenses connected with efforts to cover up the affair. Nixon denied any personal involvement, but the courts forced him to yield tape recordings which indicated that he had, in fact, tried to divert the investigation. Faced with what seemed almost certain impeachment, Nixon resigned.

Other leaders had the opportunity to learn from Nixon's experience. However, William Jefferson Clinton, the 42nd President, apparently did not learn from the Watergate affair the importance of telling the truth. Elected in 1992, Clinton was the youngest man elected President since John F. Kennedy in 1960. Clinton accomplished much for the national economy in his first term, and the American people showed their confidence in him by re-electing him to a second term in 1996. Prior to assuming the office of President, Clinton had been plagued with allegations about misconduct in his public and private life. In January 1998, news broke of an affair between Clinton and Monica Lewinsky, a White House intern, and a possible attempt to obstruct an independent counsel's inquiry into that affair. At a January child-care news conference in the White House, the President said, "I want to say one thing to the American people. I want you to listen to me. I'm going to say this again. I did not have sexual relations with that woman, Miss Lewinsky. I never told anybody to lie. Not a single time. Never. These allegations are false ..."

Seven months later, in an August address to the nation, Clinton admitted that he had misled the American people and that he had engaged in an inappropriate relationship with Miss Lewinsky. Clinton's conduct and his efforts to conceal his actions almost cost him the Presidency. The House of Representatives voted to impeach him on articles of perjury and obstruction of justice. Clinton subsequently was acquitted of the charges in a Senate trial.

Newspaper articles following Clinton's acquittal quoted one senator as predicting that Clinton would go down in history as the most accomplished, polished liar ever elected to the White House. The very name Clinton, the senator forecast, will become part of the lexicon as "a synonym for an elegant, well-crafted lie." That's a sad legacy for someone who promised the nation a brighter tomorrow and did so much to improve the American economy during his years in office.

Both Nixon and Clinton would have fared better if they had remembered the Biblical commandment, "Thou shalt not bear false witness." Their legacies would have been vastly different.

Not only do our lies hurt us, they also hurt other people. Tom lost his driving privileges because of me. Some of Clinton's top aides were furious because he had lied to them. His wife and daughter were left with a legacy of pain, anger, humiliation and embarrassment that will endure for years to come. And it was not only the Clintons, but also the American people, who were left holding the bag for tremendous legal bills.

Trust is basic to all endeavors. Where there is no trust, there is no team spirit. Tell the truth; it's a lot easier to remember, and it will almost never trap you in an untenable situation.

Chapter Fourteen
Commandment 12:
Practice The Golden Rule

Most of us have heard this directive all our lives: Treat others as you would like to be treated. We have memorized the words, but what this commandment is asking us to do is to put them into practice. As you are in the workplace, working with your team, I urge you to treat them as you would like to be treated, always sending the message, "I care about you. You are important. You are appreciated."

Unfortunately there is a handful of people who seem to follow one erstwhile comedian's misappropriation of The Golden Rule: "Do unto others, then cut out." They believe in putting themselves first, and not caring what follows.

Andrew Carnegie, who made millions and millions of dollars in the steel industry, learned at an early age the wisdom of treating others as he would wish to be treated, to reward effort with more than a monetary return. When he was a youngster, Carnegie's parents gave him two rabbits — one male and one female. You know what happened next: Lots of baby rabbits. But Carnegie had no money to buy food for all those baby rabbits. So, he enlisted the aid of his young friends. He told them that if they would go out each day and help him pull enough clover and dandelions to feed his burgeoning livestock, he would name the bunnies in their honor. His plan worked like magic. In later years, Carnegie used a similar strategy to entice railroad people to buy steel rails from him: He named his steel mills after his customers. Flattered, they remained his customers.

At Stone's Drug Store, where I worked through my senior year in high school, we were required to master two rules: Rule One was, "The customer is always right." Rule Two was, "If the customer is not right, re-read Rule One." While it sometimes took a lot of tongue-biting (even then I was never known to fail to say what I thought), I soon learned that a satisfied customer is a continuing customer and your best advertisement.

A few years ago, the only supermarket in a downtown area of Richmond, Virginia, announced its impending closing. The reason? Not enough customers to render continued operation profitable. But Johnny Johnson, a young minority businessman, understanding the plight of area residents, many of whom were without private transportation and were on fixed incomes, made arrangements to buy the

The Twelve Commandments

store. With widespread publicity and the support of residents of that urban neighborhood, Johnson reopened the market, continued serving what a larger commercial operation had termed an unprofitable population, and then expanded throughout other similar neighborhoods. In addition to subsequently making his own fortune, he enabled less-economically fortunate residents to keep their pride and self-sufficiency. He named his corporation Community Pride, and his customers repaid him with their loyalty and their money.

Mary Kay Ash, founder and chairman emeritus of Mary Kay Inc., used the Golden Rule as her guiding philosophy. She encouraged her employees and sales force members to prioritize their lives according to a simple but empowering motto: God first, family second, career third. Today, Mary Kay Inc. has grown from a small direct-sales company to the largest direct seller of skin care products in the United States. The company has more than 500,000 independent beauty consultants in twenty-six countries worldwide and has been featured in all three editions of *The 100 Best Companies to Work for in America*. Mary Kay Ash continues to use the Golden Rule in pursuing her goal of helping women everywhere achieve their full potential.

In the workplace, we must remember that one member's problem affects the entire team; unless you all work together to solve the problem, failure is almost inevitable. Remember the story of the mule Dooley. Whatever kind of ditch you get into in the workplace, you will need others to help you, others to stand beside you, to give you support, to help pull you out. The team, working together, ensures success.

Chapter Fifteen
How To Nurture Your Own Team Spirit

Everybody gets discouraged. Everybody has bad days, days when they want to slam the door after a hard day's work, kick the dog, yell at the children, not speak to the spouse, sit in a closet and cry. Yes, even guys. But we have to be our own best cheerleaders, even when we're not in the mood.

Something I have found to be helpful as a mood-lifter is the creation and examination of a "sunshine file." In July of 1988, my good friend, Ginger Cox, adapted this idea she gleaned from a state conference meeting, and she gives one to new employees as a welcome to her school. Although she has varied the poems' verses through the years, you are invited to use it yourself. To make a sunshine file, get a bright yellow file folder or yellow pocket file. Then copy the following poem on the outside of the folder or file:

Sunshine File

Here is a special file indeed,
> To read whene'er you feel the need.
Just put in things which give you hope,
> What makes you smile and helps you cope.

When things go wrong and nothing's right
> What should you do — run home or fight?
No! Peek inside, read, rest, and grin.
> Throw out the doubt, let the sunshine in.

The file is meant to be just what it proclaims itself to be. It's a repository of items that make you feel good about yourself, items that will make the sun shine on your rainy day. This is where you should keep nice letters that you have received, cards that have cheered you, copies of poems you have read and consider worth re-reading, newspaper clippings that have highlighted your work, notes of congratulations on jobs well done, snapshots of personally- important events and people — anything that lifts your spirit.

Your sunshine file may sit unnoticed in your file cabinet or desk drawer for weeks, but it will always be there when you need it. Usually just a brief glance will refresh your lagging spirits, and its presence will encourage you to clip, collect and file additional items from time to time.

There is no specific list of items for me to suggest that you collect; they will be whatever brings a smile to your face, a bounce to your step, a sense of worth and well-being to your day. Your sunshine file, the same as your life or your work, should be what you want it to be, what you want to make of it.

And it doesn't even have to be a file. A friend uses a couple of shelves in a bookcase in her office to display her "tacky souvenir collection." The criteria for an item to make this shelf is that it not only has to be tacky, it also has to have been cheap. "You can buy 'expensive tacky' everywhere; 'cheap tacky' is hard to find," she explains. And that's what makes her collection fun.

Among her souvenirs are an Oscar Mayer weiner whistle, given to her by the driver of an official Weinermobile; a putrid-green plastic replica of the Statue of Liberty which she purchased in New York; a plastic gondola with a gondolier minus an oar (it was made that way) brought by a friend from Venice; an official red plastic Alabama back scratcher; a tin cup bearing the legend "Alcatraz"; glass beads from a New Orleans Mardi Gras; a hand-painted tile from Bethlehem with the greeting, "Shalom, Y'all" (she says the friend who bought this said that when he saw it, he immediately thought of her, and she didn't know whether to laugh or be insulted); toy cars from Kids Meals; and much more. Her colleagues enjoy exploring the shelves and laughing over the items displayed and soon they are helping her to add to it, so she gets the extra pleasure of later saying, "This was given to me by so-and-so."

She explains, "It just kind of grew, and now I

really have more items than I have room to display, so I change them about every so often. People say they have fun playing with my 'toys' and, believe it or not, I went to a public relations conference last year where a speaker advocated keeping a toy box in your office to encourage colleagues to take a 'time-out' and enjoy themselves. I guess I was just ahead of the curve on that."

And occasionally, when someone especially admires an item on the shelf, she gives it to the admirer with the admonition to take care of it and enjoy it and remember her with laughter. So far, she says it's worked like a charm. "Life is too short not to laugh as much as we can," she adds. "This is one way I can get people to laugh with me."

Dennis Nowicki, then police chief in Charlotte, North Carolina, was quoted in a January 11, 1999, Charlotte *Observer* article as saying, "... there is a role for humor in everyday life and everyday work." Nowicki said that in his 35 years in law enforcement, he had experienced many situations where humor had helped accomplish a goal. He pointed out that in addition to its many healthful and stress-relieving benefits, humor can be a valuable tool for police officers in defusing violent situations.

Nowicki had arranged for John Andrews and Bill Waters, two Northern Michigan University criminal justice professors, to conduct a workshop for Charlotte-Mecklenburg officers and supervisors, on the science behind humor and ways it can improve dealings with other officers and the public. During the workshop, the professors shared these tidbits:

•A survey of corporate vice presidents and human resource managers found 84 percent think employees who have a sense of humor do a better job.

•Adults laugh an average of 15 times a day. Children laugh between 350 and 400 times a day.

•A study found that 100 laughs produce the same aerobic benefits as 10 minutes on a rowing machine or 15 minutes on a stationary bike.

•Laughter has been shown to lower blood pressure, stimulate endorphins and strengthen the immune system. One good belly laugh reduces tension for about 45 minutes.

Humor, used correctly, performs valuable services in our workplaces and in our personal lives. It not only lifts our spirits, it helps us communicate a sense of well-being to others.

Actor Michael Landon, star of "Bonanza" and "Little House on the Prairie," who died too young, left these poignant words that should inspire us: "Somebody should tell us, right at the start of our lives, that we are dying. Then we might live life to the limit, every minute of every day. Do it! I say. Whatever you want to do, do it now! There are only so many tomorrows."

Instead of reading that as a death knell, we should resolve right now to treat each day as a new beginning, to see a new world of opportunity with each dawn. I learned the inevitability of death early, with the passing of a classmate of mine, Little Eb, but I consider myself fortunate to have gained that knowledge at a tender age.

It would be wonderful if life were a video game that we could play over and over, adjusting our hand-eye coordination here and our thought-speech processes there, until we got it just right. But life is not a video game- although I sometimes feel like I'm caught in a pinball machine. Each of us gets just one chance at life. The good news, however, is that life is better than a video game. Because we haven't encountered the same pre-programmed set of circumstances before, each challenge is new and exciting. We have the power. We are in control. We can choose our own attitude.

Walter D. Wintl offers his thoughts in the following poem:

Defeatism

If you think you're beaten, you are,
If you think you dare not, you don't,
If you'd like to win, but think you can't,
It is almost a cinch you won't.
If you think you'll lose, you've lost,
For out in the world you'll find
Success begins in a fellow's will
It is all in the state of mind.
For many a race is lost
Before ever a step is run.
And many a coward fails
Before his work's begun.
Think big, and your deeds will rise:
Think small, and you'll fall behind.
Think that you can and you will.
It is all in the state of mind.
If you think you're outclassed, you are:
You've got to think high to rise,
You've got to be sure of yourself,

Before you can ever win a prize.
Life's battles don't always go
To the stronger or faster man,
But sooner or later the man who wins,
Is the fellow who thinks he can.

Every night before I sleep, I thank God for the many blessings of life, and for my family and friends who have enriched my life. Then I ask for His forgiveness for my mistakes and His guidance for the days ahead. I try to think of things that I have done that day of which I am proud. Then I recall where I have fallen short and made mistakes. I try to understand where I went wrong so I won't be doomed to repetition. Then, I vow to start afresh, putting my experiences, knowledge and new understanding to use, to fill the next day's slate with spirit and laughter and productivity.

Even when we work alone, we are part of a greater team, and we must remember the commandments for people who work with people. Our observance of those commandments, along with the observance of a Greater Ten, will ensure our success in work and our happiness in life.

About The Author

Dr. Ann Threadgill White was born in Cherokee County, South Carolina. Later her family moved to Spartanburg County where she continues to make her home. Ann grew up watching "I Love Lucy," and enjoyed this program so much that she wanted to be funny like Lucy. In school, she was always telling funny stories to her friends and teachers. As a young girl, she learned to love entertaining others. She put her gift of humor to use during her first career in education, beginning as a classroom teacher, progressing to a library media specialist, then a public information director, and ending as an assistant superintendent of personnel.

Today, she uses that gift even more in her second career as a professional speaker, humorist and consultant through her business, *Laugh And Learn With Ann White*. She has been published in a variety of professional journals and travels across North and Central America, speaking to audiences ranging from teenagers to corporate leaders, inspiring them to meet the challenges of their public and private lives.

Ann White received her bachelor's degree in social studies from Limestone College in Gaffney, South Carolina; a master's degree in secondary school counseling from the University of South Carolina; and a doctorate of education in school administration from Nova Southeastern University. She is a member of numerous national and state organizations including the National Speakers Association, the Carolinas Speakers Association, American Business Women's Association, Altrusa International, Phi Delta Kappa, the South Carolina Association of School Librarians and the South Carolina Association of School Administrators. She is a past president of the South Carolina Association of Allied School Administrators and the South Carolina Association of School Librarians. Among her many honors and awards she has been named Communicator of Achievement by Media Women of South Carolina, an affiliate of the National Federation of Press Women, and received the Distinguished Service Award from the South Carolina Association of School Librarians.

Ann and her husband, William, who is the mayor of Cowpens, South Carolina, have three children and one grandchild. They have two cats, Doodle and Sable.

About The Editor

Frances Helms, a native of Cherokee County, South Carolina, is a national and state award-winning writer and editor for books, newspapers and magazines. She studied music and education at Limestone College in Gaffney, South Carolina, and English and psychology at Converse College in Spartanburg, South Carolina, before earning a Master of Arts in Journalism from the University of South Carolina. She has presented numerous workshops on writing and editing, has been an adjunct professor in journalism at the University of South Carolina at Spartanburg, and has been a volunteer career counselor for the Women's Resource Center at the University of Richmond (Virginia). For five years she wrote a weekly column that was distributed worldwide by the New York Times News Service.

The mother of four and stepmother of one, she is married to Dr. Vance Helms, a human resources director. They have ten grandchildren.

After collaborating with Ann White on this book, she remains a friend.

For information regarding speeches and seminars, Ann White may be reached at (864)463-6709 or Drawer 1019 Cowpens, SC 29330. For her latest topics go to www.annwhite.com Listed below is a sample of some favorite topics of her many audiences.

Twelve Commandments for People Who Work With People

A memorable keynote address that contains substance wrapped with humor. It is packed with ideas for improving interpersonal relationships with customers, associates, staff and family.

You Are Only the Person You Let Yourself Be

A humorous, side-splitting keynote address highlighting the behaviors and abilities we have control over in our lives. Filled with substance on dealing with change, the power of attitude, making good choices, and using humor and past experiences to improve our spirits and leadership skills.

Keeping Spirits High

This fun-filled presentation emphasizes the key components for making today's workplace a place of joy. It shows how a dose of humor can increase low morale, improve the wellness of employees and lead to greater profits and productivity.

Perceiving Is Believing

A lively presentation about how people get perceptions of businesses, organizations, agencies and any group that serves people. Humorous stories are used to illustrate the impact of personality, body language, personal experience, influence of others and the print and non print media on perceptions. Most importantly, the secrets of changing perceptions are shared.

To order additional copies of this book, posters and tapes, photo-copy this page and mail to Ann White at Drawer 1019, Cowpens, SC 29330 or fax your order form to (864)463-9909.

Name_____

Mailing Address _____

_____ Zip Code_____

Shipping Address _____

_____ Zip Code_____

Call or write for discounts on bulk orders.

Please send a check or money order with orders less than $50. Other orders will be billed.

Purchase Order No. _____

I wish to order the following Item(s):

Book *Twelve Commandments for People Who Work With People* $11.95 each *(add $3.20 for shipping and handling)*

Quantity	Unit Price	Total
	$11.95	

Poster Twelve Commandments for People Who Work With People $7.00 each *(add $2.00 for shipping and handling)*.

Quantity	Unit Price	Total
	$7.00	

Audio tape "Twelve Commandments for People Who Work With People" — $10.00 each *(add $1.50 for shipping and handling)*. Please choose the edition you would like.

Edition	Quantity	Unit Price	Total
Business/Industry		**$10.00**	
Teachers		**$10.00**	
Librarians/Media Professionals		**$10.00**	

Total for all items   _____

South Carolina residents add 5% sales tax   _____

Shipping & Handling   _____

Total_____